EARTHQUAKES

© Aladdin Books Ltd 1992

Designed and produced by
Aladdin Books Ltd
28 Percy Street
London W1P 9FF

First published in
Great Britain in 1992 by
Gloucester Press Ltd
96 Leonard Street
London EC2A 4RH

Design: David West
            Children's Book
            Design
Designer: Stephen Woosnam-Savage
Editor: Fiona Robertson
Illustrator: Mike Saunders
Researcher: Emma Krikler

ISBN 0 7496 0759 9

Printed in Belgium

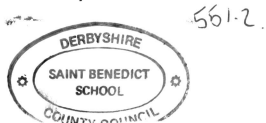

Natural Disasters

EARTHQUAKES

JANE WALKER

GLOUCESTER PRESS
London · New York · Toronto · Sydney

CONTENTS

INTRODUCTION

The destructive power of an earthquake is one of the most violent and deadly of all natural forces. In just a few seconds, these massive vibrations of the Earth's crust can shatter whole communities. The earthquakes unleashed on some of the world's most densely populated areas are not necessarily the largest. Yet they cause the greatest amount of damage and the highest number of deaths. Scientists hope to avoid such devastating losses by developing more accurate methods of earthquake prediction.

WHAT IS AN EARTHQUAKE?

An earthquake is the sudden, and often violent, trembling of part of the Earth's surface. It sends shock waves racing through the Earth's crust, which is the name given to the rocky outer layer surrounding the Earth. Earthquakes are generated in the huge tile-like sections, called plates, which make up this crust.

A plate boundary is the area where two of these plates meet. Continual movement at plate boundaries creates a build-up of pressure beneath the surface. Rocks are elastic up to a point and can absorb the strain from

this pressure for hundreds, even thousands, of years. Eventually, however, they snap, or rupture, at their weakest point, relieving the enormous strain. Huge amounts of energy are released as shock waves, called seismic waves, radiate outwards from the point where the rocks fractured. The area within the Earth's crust where the shock waves begin is called the earthquake's focus. The place on the surface directly above the focus is the epicentre.

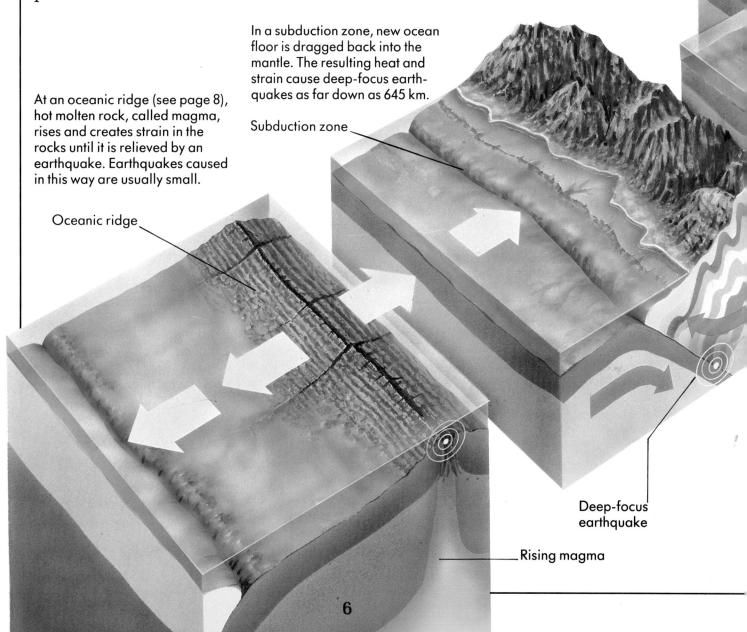

In a subduction zone, new ocean floor is dragged back into the mantle. The resulting heat and strain cause deep-focus earthquakes as far down as 645 km.

Subduction zone

At an oceanic ridge (see page 8), hot molten rock, called magma, rises and creates strain in the rocks until it is relieved by an earthquake. Earthquakes caused in this way are usually small.

Oceanic ridge

Deep-focus earthquake

Rising magma

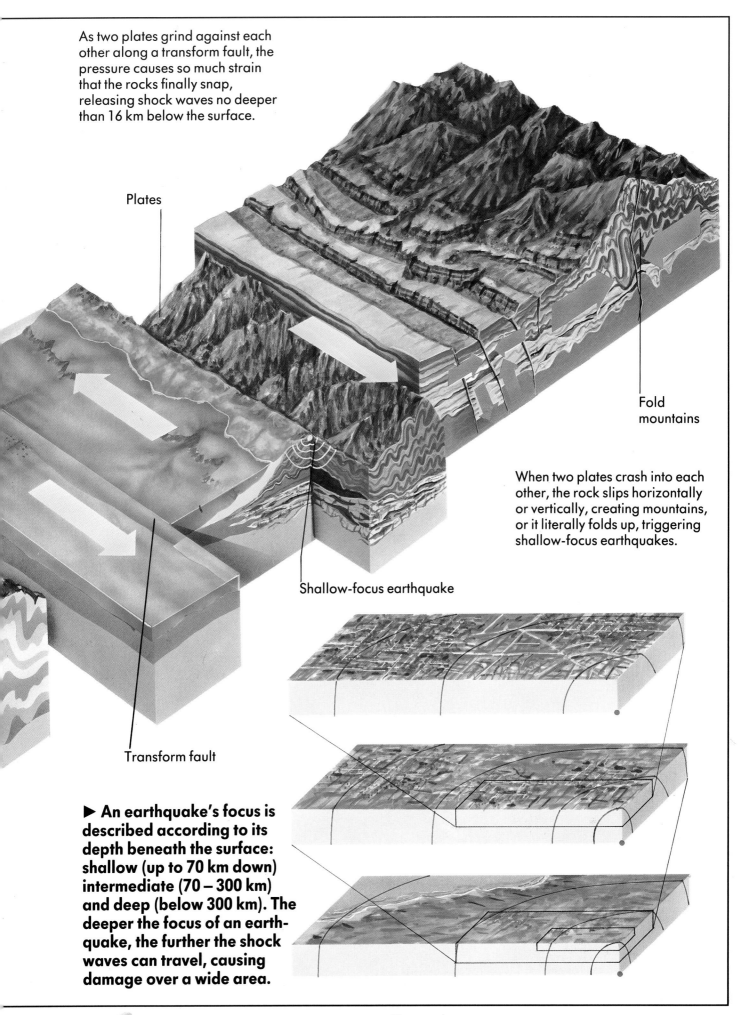

As two plates grind against each other along a transform fault, the pressure causes so much strain that the rocks finally snap, releasing shock waves no deeper than 16 km below the surface.

Plates

Fold mountains

When two plates crash into each other, the rock slips horizontally or vertically, creating mountains, or it literally folds up, triggering shallow-focus earthquakes.

Shallow-focus earthquake

Transform fault

▶ **An earthquake's focus is described according to its depth beneath the surface: shallow (up to 70 km down) intermediate (70 – 300 km) and deep (below 300 km). The deeper the focus of an earthquake, the further the shock waves can travel, causing damage over a wide area.**

THE MOVING EARTH

The Earth consists of three separate layers: the crust, the mantle and the core. The crust is made of giant plates which are constantly moving. The plates float in the hot molten rock, called magma, of the upper mantle. Pressure in the mantle forces the magma up through the crust along the oceanic ridges. These areas are known as constructive plate margins because when the magma cools and hardens, it forms new ocean floor.

In subduction zones, or destructive plate margins, ocean floor is destroyed when plates collide and the edge of one plate is dragged down into the mantle. At a third type of boundary, the transform fault, plates are simply sliding past each other, and so the fault is neither a constructive nor a destructive boundary. Plate movements at all three types of boundary can give rise to earthquakes.

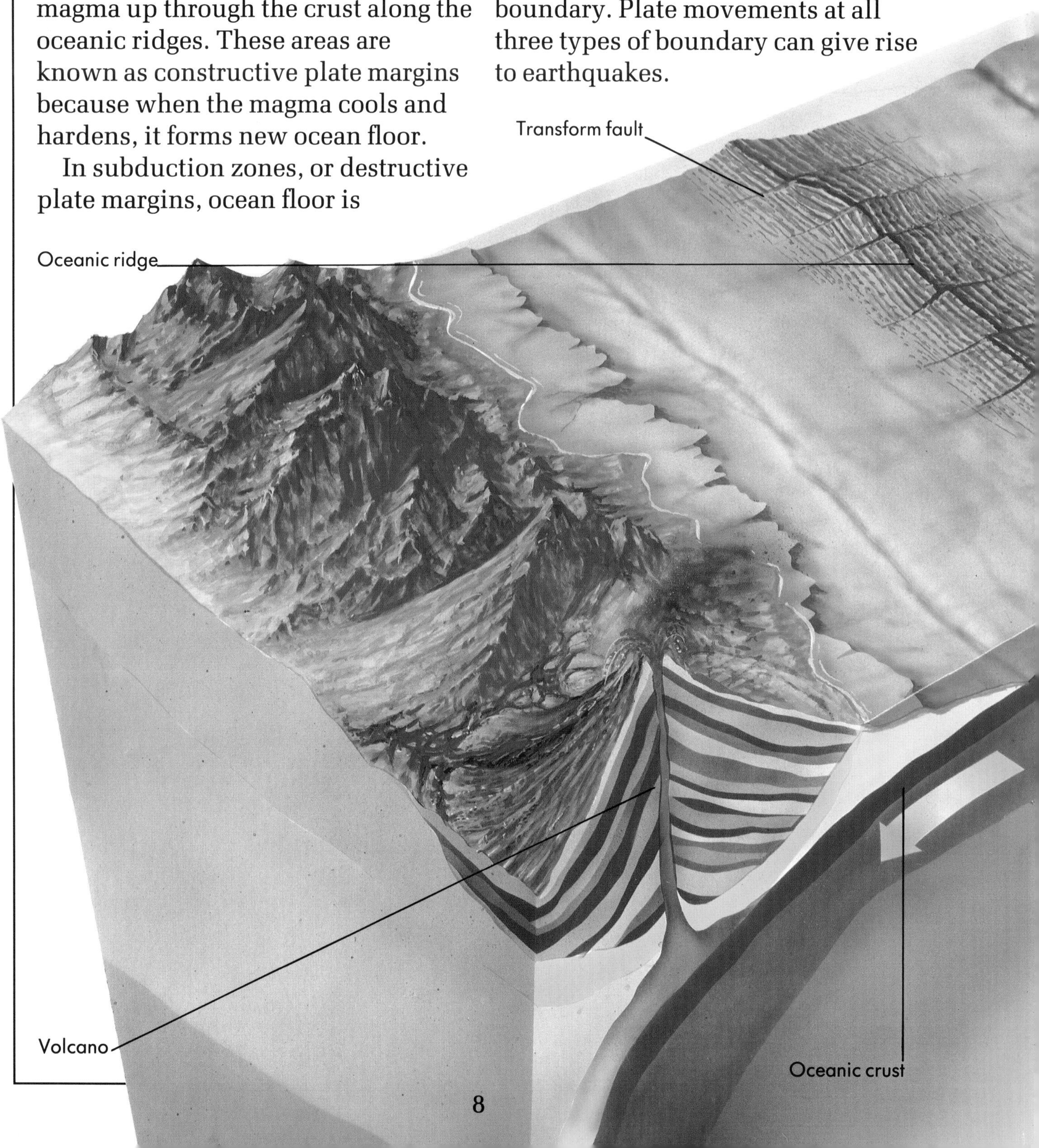

Transform fault

Oceanic ridge

Volcano

Oceanic crust

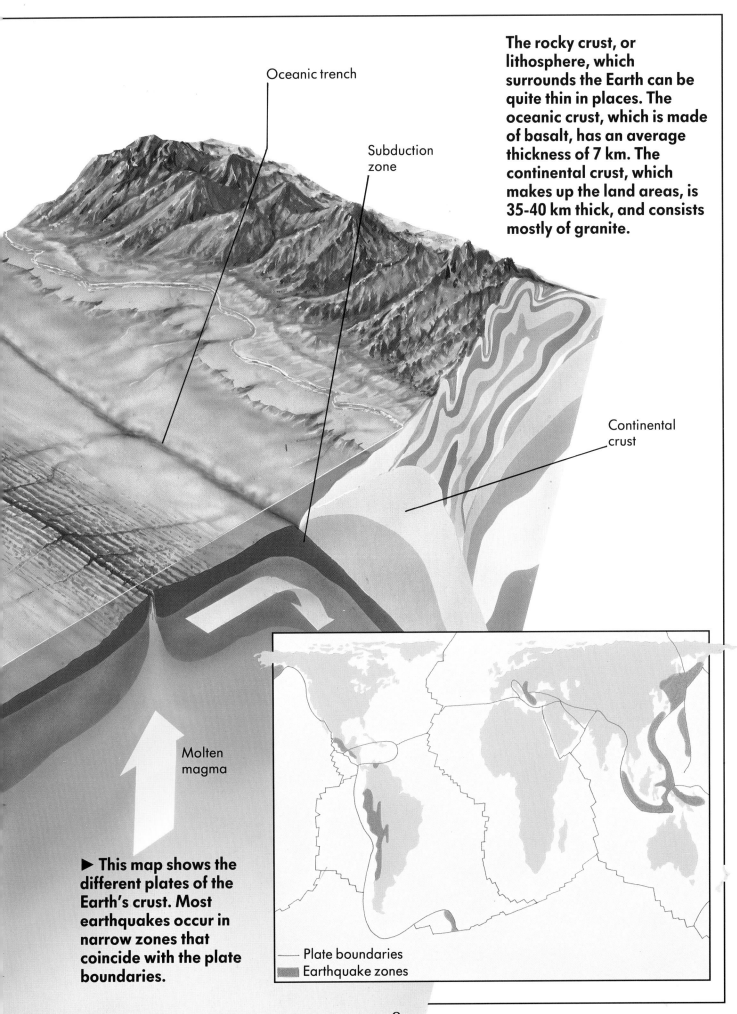

Oceanic trench

Subduction zone

The rocky crust, or lithosphere, which surrounds the Earth can be quite thin in places. The oceanic crust, which is made of basalt, has an average thickness of 7 km. The continental crust, which makes up the land areas, is 35-40 km thick, and consists mostly of granite.

Continental crust

Molten magma

► This map shows the different plates of the Earth's crust. Most earthquakes occur in narrow zones that coincide with the plate boundaries.

—— Plate boundaries

▓▓ Earthquake zones

9

AN EARTHQUAKE BEGINS

In the period before an earthquake, the pressure building up in the rock layers beneath the ground causes so much strain that cracks appear in walls and pavements. When the rocks finally snap, the first seismic waves to be released from the earthquake's focus are known as body waves. Body waves travel through the Earth and are of two types: primary (P) and secondary (S) waves. Waves that only travel along the surface of the Earth are surface, or long (L), waves.

Primary waves travel through solid rock, volcanic lava, water and even air at speeds of up to 8 km per second. P waves are followed by S waves, which travel more slowly at about 6 km per second. When the body waves reach the surface, some are transformed into surface waves. Surface waves produce the most severe ground movements. A violent jolt is felt at the epicentre as the ground moves. The first tremor may last for only 30-60 seconds, but further tremors, or aftershocks, occur soon after as the disturbed rocks settle into a new position.

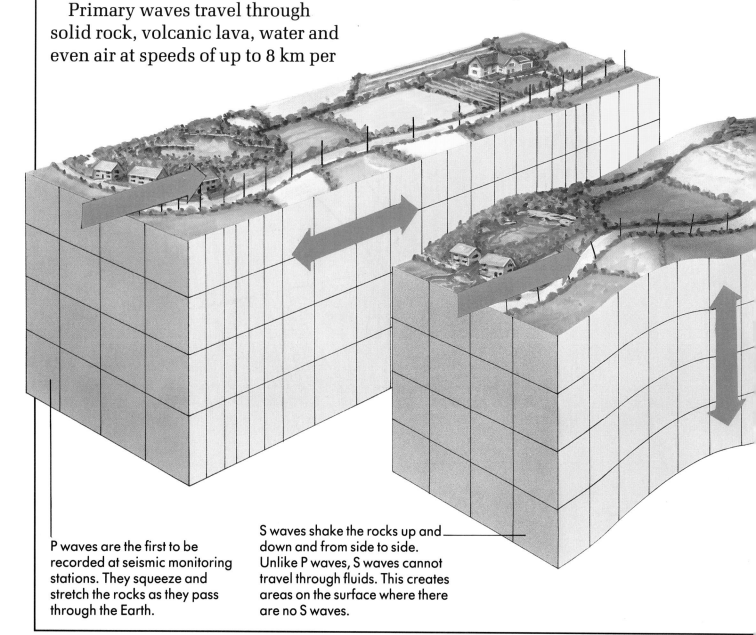

P waves are the first to be recorded at seismic monitoring stations. They squeeze and stretch the rocks as they pass through the Earth.

S waves shake the rocks up and down and from side to side. Unlike P waves, S waves cannot travel through fluids. This creates areas on the surface where there are no S waves.

Telltale signs

Certain warning signs have been noticed before an earthquake. Minor tremors make the ground shake gently. As the rocks beneath begin to warp and bulge, swellings appear on the surface. They cause the ground to crack and finally burst open (shown right). Scientists in China have noticed that water in ponds and canals gives off strange smells, possibly due to gas building up underground.

Rayleigh waves travel across the Earth's surface with an up-and-down rolling movement, like ocean waves. They travel at about 4 km per second.

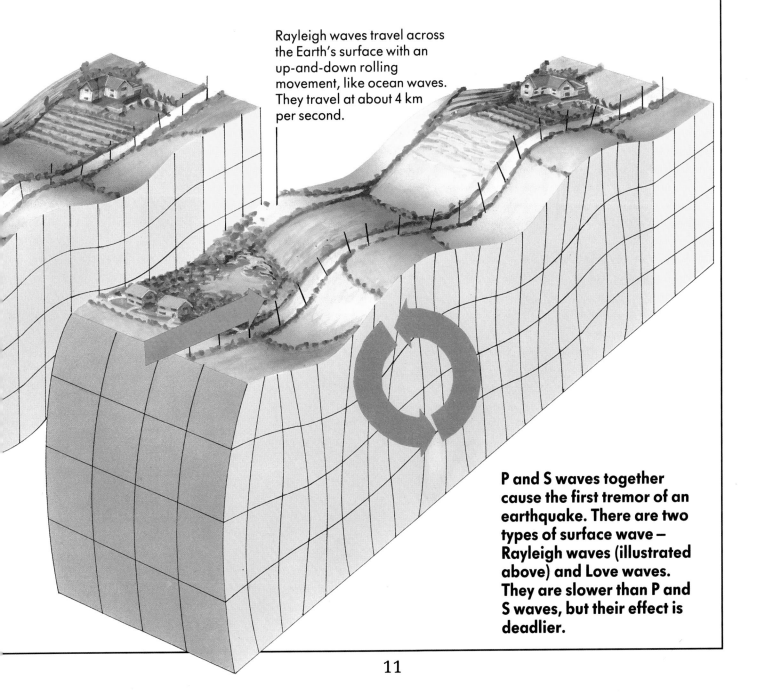

P and S waves together cause the first tremor of an earthquake. There are two types of surface wave – Rayleigh waves (illustrated above) and Love waves. They are slower than P and S waves, but their effect is deadlier.

DEATH AND DESTRUCTION

As the roar and violent motion of a major earthquake are heard and felt, tall apartment buildings and office blocks often collapse in vast piles of rubble, burying hundreds of people. In Mexico City in 1985, the main tower of the Benito Juárez Hospital collapsed floor by floor, killing 1,000 patients and staff. Huge cracks appear as roads and pavements are ripped apart, and road and rail links to the stricken area are often cut off, making it difficult for rescue workers to bring help. There is also a serious risk of fire from damaged electricity cables and gas pipes.

Earthquakes bring with them other deadly after-effects. Those that occur under the sea create giant waves, called *tsunamis*, which sweep in from the sea and lash the coast. The 1964 Alaskan quake created a *tsunami*, 21 m high in places, which raced towards Hawaii at over 645 km/h. Strong tremors cause nearby rivers to overflow, and dams and reservoirs to burst, triggering off huge landslides. An earthquake in Peru in 1971 caused a massive chunk of ice to break off Mt Huascarán in the Andes Mountains. As the ice melted, it turned into an 80 m-high mudflow which swept through the town of Yungay, killing 50,000 people.

Before and after

Mexico City (below), is built on layers of mud, clay, gravel and sand of a dried-up lake bed. Soil levels and buildings there can subside by up to 15 cm a year. Cities built on soft surfaces suffer most earthquake damage because the soft soil increases the effects of the seismic waves.

Amazingly, the 52-storey headquarters of Mexico's state oil company, the tallest tower in Latin America, survived the shock waves of the 1985 earthquake. With the aid of special equipment, several dozen babies were rescued alive from the ruins of the city's hospitals.

► After the 1989 earth-quake in San Francisco (63 dead and 4,000 injured), losses across the city totalled US $6,000 million.

▼ The earthquake in the Indian state of Uttar Pradesh on 20 October 1991 caused widespread structural damage to bridges and roads.

MEASURING EARTHQUAKES

The scientists who study the seismic waves released from the focus of an earthquake are called seismologists. Special measuring instruments, called seismographs, record the pattern of the seismic waves. Seismologists use these patterns to determine the strength and duration of an earthquake, as well as the amount of movement along a fault line. Taking readings at several different points on the Earth's surface also helps them to pinpoint the exact location of the earthquake's focus.

Two different scales are used to measure the strength of an earthquake. The most common one is the Richter Scale, devised by an American seismologist, Charles Richter, in 1935. It calculates the magnitude of an earthquake from seismograph recordings that measure the amount of energy released. An increase of 1 point on the Richter Scale means that an earthquake is 10 times stronger than one with the next value below. An earthquake measuring less than 5 on the Richter Scale causes minimal damage, while a major earthquake measures 7 or more. The second scale is the Mercalli Scale, which calculates the intensity of an earthquake by assessing the damage it causes.

I: Felt by only a very few people. II: Felt by a few, on upper floors.

III: Similar to a passing vehicle.
IV: Felt by many people indoors.

V: Buildings tremble and trees shake.
VI: Felt by all. Plaster cracks.

VII: Bricks loosen. Difficult to stand. VIII: Damage to weak structures.

▶ **Jagged tracings (right) are made as the seismograph records the movements of the ground during an earthquake. Scientists can distinguish between the primary, secondary and surface waves.**

IX: Pipes crack. Buildings collapse. X: Huge ground cracks. Landslides.

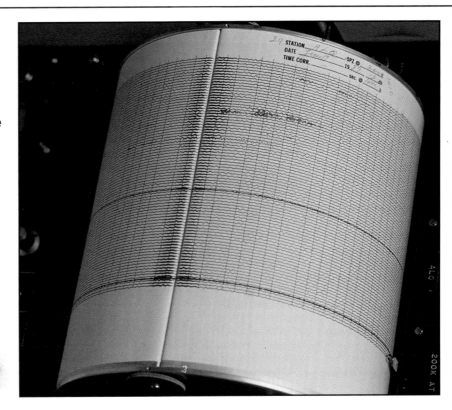

◀ **The Mercalli Scale was invented in 1902 by an Italian seismologist, Giuseppe Mercalli, and modified during the 1930s by American scientists. The scale describes effects that range from tiny swaying movements (I) to total devastation (XII).**

XI: Most buildings destroyed. *Tsunamis*. XII: Total destruction. Surface waves seen.

Seismographs

One type of seismograph records the horizontal movements of the Earth, and the other type records the vertical movements. A weight is attached to a frame by a sensitive spring. As the ground trembles, the weight remains stationary but the frame moves and a pen records the movement on paper wrapped around a rotating drum. This recording is called a seismogram.

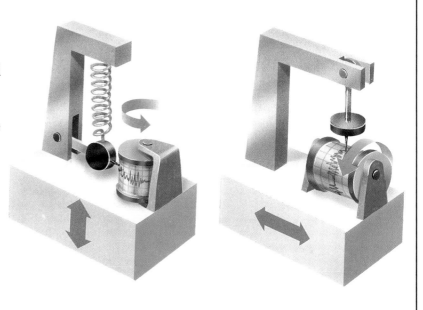

EARTHQUAKES IN HISTORY

Many of the myths and legends surrounding earthquakes date back thousands of years. Some of the world's greatest civilizations have been built up around major earthquake zones such as China, the mountainous areas of the Middle East, Mexico, and the lands around the Mediterranean Sea and India.

Primitive peoples believed that earthquakes were caused by the actions of huge beasts. Hindu mythology claimed that the Earth was supported by eight huge elephants. When one of the elephants became tired and lowered and shook its head, this resulted in an earthquake. According to Japanese legend, earthquakes are caused by the *namazu*, a giant catfish living in the mud beneath the Earth's surface. The *namazu* is something of a prankster who can only be controlled by the Kashima god. In October 1855, when the gods were said to be visiting a distant shrine, an earthquake struck the city of Edo (modern Tokyo). In the absence of the Kashima god, the catfish had hurled itself around and unleashed the earthquake.

▼ **The Japanese legend of the *namazu* was depicted in many popular 19th-century prints. The one below shows the people of Edo attacking the *namazu* for unleashing the earthquake.**

The first earthquake sensor

This instrument was designed by the Chinese in the 2nd century AD. During a tremor, a swinging weight opened the mouth of one of eight dragons. A small bronze ball dropped from the dragon's mouth onto the open-mouthed frog below, making a loud clang. The dragon with the empty mouth indicated the direction of the earthquake.

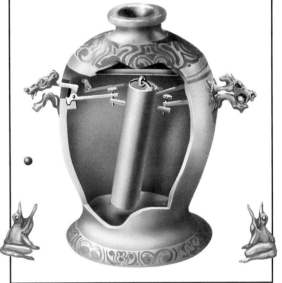

▲ The earthquake which devastated the Jamaican city of Port Royal (above) in 1692 left 2,000 people dead. Port Royal was an important pirate centre for the West Indies, trading in slaves and rum. Many people believed that the earthquake was a punishment from God.

▶ This engraving shows one of the effects of the earthquake which struck the Calabria region of southern Italy in 1783. About 50,000 people died in a series of earthquakes over a 7-week period. Later, the Academy of Sciences and Fine Letters in Naples set up a commission to assess the damage.

THE LISBON EARTHQUAKE

On the morning of All Saints' Day, 1 November 1755, in the city of Lisbon, capital of the Portuguese empire, many of the city's inhabitants were in church. At 9.40 am, everything began to shudder violently as the first shock waves of an earthquake reached the city. Buildings rocked from side to side, and the spires of the city's many churches swayed. In terror, worshippers in the cathedral of Santa Maria rushed out into the nearby square, only to be crushed to death as a second, more violent tremor caused the cathedral to collapse, along with much of the rest of the city.

As the first tremors subsided, fire threatened to engulf the city as timber and furniture collapsed into fireplaces and set alight. Huge sea waves swept over the quaysides, sucking up people, masonry, ships and animals. About 60,000 people died in Lisbon that morning. Tremors were observed as far away as Sweden and Scotland, and in Spain and North Africa thousands more died as buildings collapsed. Scientists have estimated that the quake would have measured 8.75 on the Richter Scale.

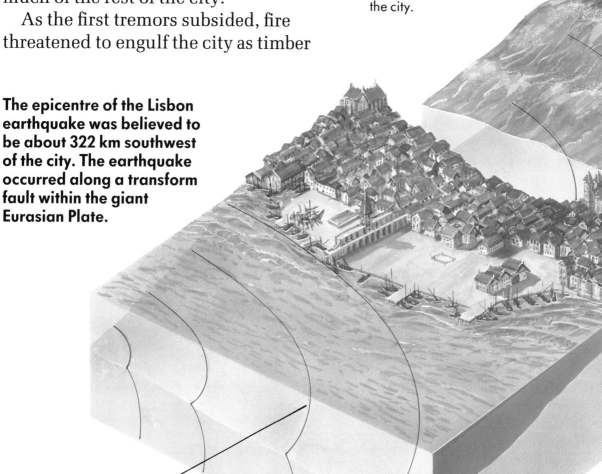

From the banks of the River Tagus, a huge 15 m wave hurled itself across the city.

The epicentre of the Lisbon earthquake was believed to be about 322 km southwest of the city. The earthquake occurred along a transform fault within the giant Eurasian Plate.

The shock waves from the first tremor travelled from the epicentre to Lisbon within seconds.

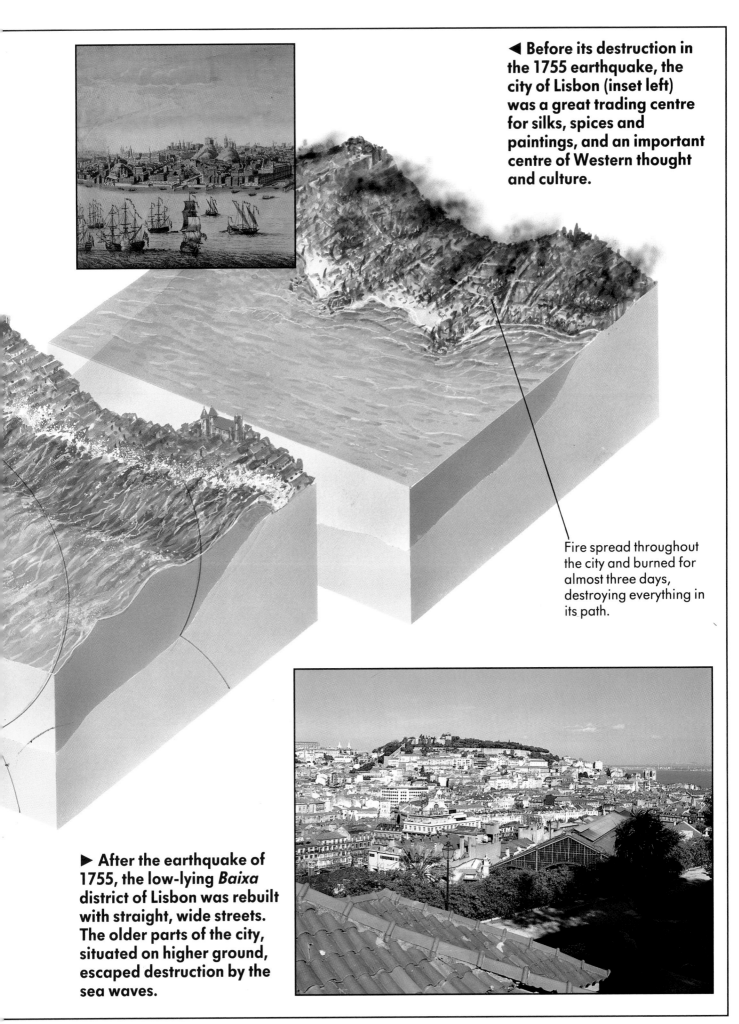

◄ Before its destruction in the 1755 earthquake, the city of Lisbon (inset left) was a great trading centre for silks, spices and paintings, and an important centre of Western thought and culture.

Fire spread throughout the city and burned for almost three days, destroying everything in its path.

► After the earthquake of 1755, the low-lying *Baixa* district of Lisbon was rebuilt with straight, wide streets. The older parts of the city, situated on higher ground, escaped destruction by the sea waves.

THE SAN ANDREAS FAULT

The giant San Andreas Fault system stretches for more than 1,210 km along the coast of California in the United States. This transform fault lies along the boundary between the Pacific Plate and the North American Plate. As these two plates constantly grind against each other, some of the resulting strain is released from time to time by tiny quakes. But when the plates become locked together, this prevents any release. The pressure builds up over a period of years until a massive quake occurs, such as the one on 18 April 1906. Although the earthquake only lasted for 40 seconds, its force (Richter Scale 8.3) was enormous. In San Francisco, 700 people died, over 28,000 buildings were ruined and over 250,000 people were left homeless.

Today, evidence of the San Andreas Fault can be seen in cracked walls and scarred landscapes (below).

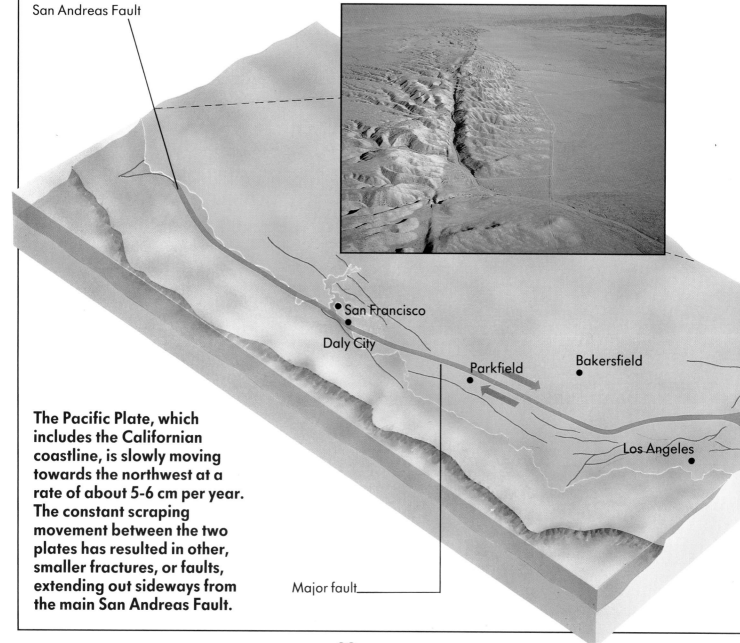

San Andreas Fault

San Francisco

Daly City

Parkfield

Bakersfield

Los Angeles

The Pacific Plate, which includes the Californian coastline, is slowly moving towards the northwest at a rate of about 5-6 cm per year. The constant scraping movement between the two plates has resulted in other, smaller fractures, or faults, extending out sideways from the main San Andreas Fault.

Major fault

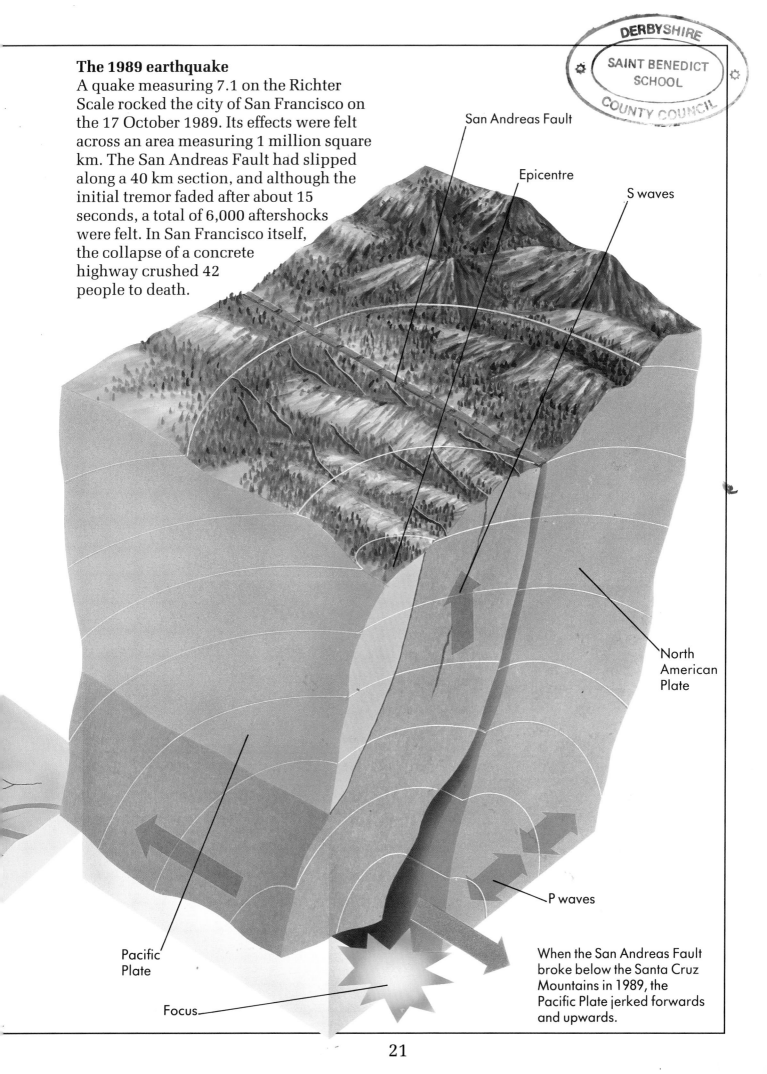

The 1989 earthquake

A quake measuring 7.1 on the Richter Scale rocked the city of San Francisco on the 17 October 1989. Its effects were felt across an area measuring 1 million square km. The San Andreas Fault had slipped along a 40 km section, and although the initial tremor faded after about 15 seconds, a total of 6,000 aftershocks were felt. In San Francisco itself, the collapse of a concrete highway crushed 42 people to death.

San Andreas Fault

Epicentre

S waves

North American Plate

P waves

Pacific Plate

Focus

When the San Andreas Fault broke below the Santa Cruz Mountains in 1989, the Pacific Plate jerked forwards and upwards.

EARTHQUAKES TODAY

Each year, an estimated 500,000 disturbances occur within the Earth's crust. Most pass unnoticed, but about 1,000 earthquakes a year cause some damage, and occasionally a major earthquake brings disaster. At 11.41 am on 7 December 1988, an earthquake (Richter Scale 7.0) struck the Republic of Armenia in the Soviet Union. The small town of Spitak lay in ruins, while in nearby Leninakan and Kirovakan, up to three-quarters of all buildings were destroyed. After an initial estimate of 55,000, the death toll was revised down to 25,000.

Deep below the surface of the Caspian Sea, on 21 June 1990, shock waves were released from the focus of an earthquake measuring between 7.3 and 7.7 on the Richter Scale. The first tremor was felt in the Iranian capital of Tehran. A second one followed 12 hours later.

In October 1991, a series of four earthquakes in northern India left more than 500 people dead and thousands injured. The most powerful quake measured 7.1 on the Richter Scale. Its epicentre was around the town of Uttarkarshi, but tremors were felt in the Indian capital of Delhi 240 km away. Rescue operations were hampered by the mountainous landscape, and by landslides which blocked a tributary of the River Ganges.

▼ A tangled heap of twisted metal and broken concrete marks the site of a 16-storey block of flats which collapsed after the 1989 earthquake in Armenia.

Relief efforts

After the recent earthquakes in the Soviet Union and Iran, huge international relief operations were mounted to help these countries handle such disasters. In Armenia, freezing winter conditions, unco-ordinated relief efforts, and damage to the area's road and rail networks hampered the rescue operation. In Iran, the mountainous terrain proved to be an obstacle in reaching people in stricken villages.

◀ After the 1985 earthquake in Mexico City (Richter Scale 8.1), a lack of basic equipment, such as cranes and saws to cut through concrete, prevented volunteers from freeing people trapped under the rubble of collapsed buildings.

◀◀ The worst effects of the 1990 Iranian earthquake centred on the towns of Binab and Abhor, both of which were destroyed. About 35,000 people were killed, and thousands more were injured.

EARTHQUAKE PREDICTION

On the afternoon of 4 February 1974, a radio broadcast to the three million inhabitants of Liaoning Province in China warned them to leave their homes immediately because of an impending earthquake. Just after 7.30 that evening, an earthquake destroyed or damaged almost all the buildings in the city of Haicheng (pop. 90,000). Miraculously, the death toll was only about 300 people. For the first time anywhere in the world an earthquake of this strength had been predicted correctly.

Seismologists have identified several warning signs in the build-up to an earthquake: alterations in the speed of seismic waves, swellings in the ground and a large number of minor tremors along the plate boundaries. With the help of modern technology, scientists can monitor even the tiniest movement in the Earth's plates. Scientists in China have relied on a number of less scientific warning signs to predict earthquakes. They claim that, before an earthquake, fish become very agitated and small animals like mice and rabbits run around in panic.

▶ **The picture on the right shows a scientist checking the equipment installed in one of 18 water wells around the town of Parkfield in the United States. Parkfield is situated along the San Andreas Fault, and scientists have predicted that an earthquake of around magnitude 6 will occur there before 1993. Dozens of researchers have made the town of Parkfield the most closely-monitored earthquake region in the world. Instruments in the wells record the level of groundwater as the rock beneath is affected by the build-up of pressure caused by seismic activity. The antenna situated on top of the equipment transmits data to a satellite which then relays the information to Parkfield Experiment Headquarters for analysis.**

► A creepmeter measures the continuous horizontal movement along a fault line. A weight on the end of a piece of wire rises or falls as the fault moves.

▼ The black "dustbin" shown below is the covering of a well containing a strain meter. Strain meters can detect even tiny rock movements. The solar panels provide energy to operate the equipment.

Laser light

The United States and Japan have been world leaders in developing new technology to help predict earthquakes. Some American monitoring stations use laser beams to detect any movement in the rocks beneath the ground. A beam of laser light is sent from one side of a fault line to a reflector positioned on the opposite side. By calculating the amount of time it takes the laser beam to bounce off the reflector, scientists can measure any movement of the ground which occurs along the fault.

TOKYO – A CITY PREPARED

Following the catastrophic effects of the 1923 earthquake in Tokyo, the Japanese saw the rebuilding of their capital city as an opportunity to plan for future earthquakes, and so avoid any further large-scale destruction.

Special regulations control the height of new buildings and the design of their internal structure. The authorities realised that they needed to protect the city's road and railway system, as well as gas and water pipes and electricity cables. To avoid the problem of a damaged water supply, making it difficult to carry out a successful fire-fighting operation, a 10-day supply of water, amounting to some 400,000 tonnes, is stored in earthquake-proof tanks in Tokyo. In addition, stockpiles of food and blankets have been prepared for the city's 8 million inhabitants.

In preparation for any future earthquake, trained disaster teams have been created, and earthquake drills are held regularly in schools, offices and factories. A constant stream of leaflets, posters and TV and radio broadcasts reminds residents about the need to be prepared. It should now be possible to give sufficient warning time, with the help of the huge bank of seismographs at the Japan Meteorological Agency.

Past earthquakes

142,000 people died in the massive earthquake (Richter Scale 8.3) which rocked Japan's Kanto Plain in 1923. Out in Sagami Bay, at the focus, the sea-bed sank 400 m. Over half a million homes were destroyed in Tokyo and Yokohama.

Ironically, Tokyo's newly-built Imperial Hotel was due to be officially opened that day. The hotel had been specially designed to withstand an earthquake. As the ceremony was about to begin, the quake smashed into Tokyo, bringing with it an 11m high *tsunami*.

▲ The Imperial Hotel was one of the few buildings left standing after the 1923 quake. However, its design later proved to be flawed, and the hotel was demolished in 1968. The latest advances in seismic engineering were used in the design of the New Imperial Hotel (above).

▲▶ These fire-fighters in Japan are tackling a fire as part of a regular earth-quake drill.

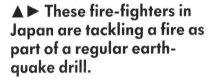

▲ Even Japanese schoolchildren are encouraged to practise earthquake drills regularly.

◀ Other earthquake-prone areas, like San Francisco (shown left), have established sophisticated emergency measures to reduce the loss of life and property during an earthquake.

WHAT CAN WE DO?

We do not yet know how to prevent earthquakes, so how can we make sure that they cause as little damage and as few deaths as possible?

Cities and towns in earthquake zones should be carefully planned and designed. Gas and water pipes and electricity cables should be well protected. In some earthquake-prone areas in the United States, electricity generators automatically shut down in the event of an earthquake, and gas pipes are closed by automatic valves. Other countries are also taking protective measures. In Iran, reinforced brick structures are replacing flat-roofed mud homes, and in Tashkent in the Soviet Union concrete buildings have replaced the brick and mud structures.

The 255m-high Transamerica Building in San Francisco (pictured below) is a monument to the success of earthquake architecture. Its triangular framework is supported by concrete-clad steel columns which should withstand even the most severe earthquake.

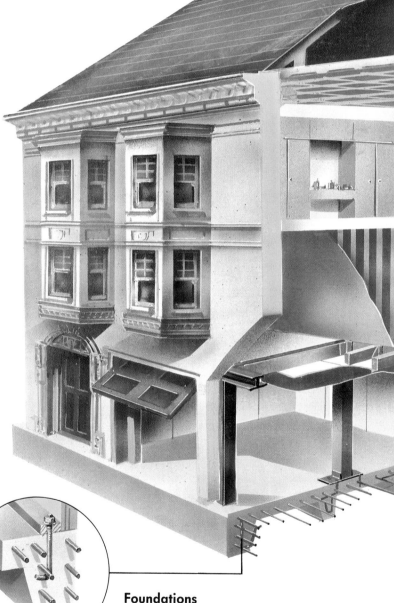

Foundations
A slab of concrete, reinforced with steel rods, will support the building. The walls are reinforced by securing them to the foundations with anchor bolts.

Chimneys
Brick chimneys must be secured with special brackets. Metal ones are lighter and cause less damage.

An earthquake-resistant house should be a low structure made of reinforced concrete. There should be strong walls on the first storey, where the effects of the quake are greatest. Foundations should be deep or flexible so that the building can sway as the ground beneath it shakes during a tremor. It is better to build on solid rock such as granite. Clay, sand and other soft surfaces increase the effects of the seismic waves.

Beams and joists
Extra reinforcement is essential where wall beams and floor joists join up. The house must be able to withstand both the vertical and the horizontal shaking movements experienced during an earthquake.

▼ The wide streets of San Francisco help to prevent the spread of fire during an earthquake, and also allow buildings to sway, without crashing into each other.

Water heater
Boilers, generators and water heaters are firmly secured to prevent them breaking loose and fracturing gas pipes.

FACT FILE

The worst death toll

The largest number of deaths from an earthquake was believed to have occurred around July 1201. The earthquake affected the Near East and eastern Mediterranean regions, leaving an estimated 1.1 million dead.

An earthquake in the Chinese city of Tangshan in 1976 measured 7.9 on the Richter Scale. The death toll was originally believed to be about 650,000, but was later reduced to 242,000 by the Chinese Government.

Largest earthquake

An earthquake measuring 8.9 on the Richter Scale struck Alaska in the United States on Good Friday, 27 March 1964. The damage caused by the quake was estimated at US $750 million. Five hours after the first tremor, a giant *tsunami* demolished the Alaskan port of Valdez, while at the oil port of Seward, a 10 m wave topped with burning oil surged across the dockside, sweeping away all the port's facilities.

Historical patterns

Scientists cannot ignore historical patterns when predicting earthquakes in some quake-prone areas. In Mexico, where five times as many earthquakes occur each year as in California, a major earthquake occurs every 35 years. The strength of the shock waves unleashed by the 1985 quake there were 1,000 times more powerful than the atomic bomb which destroyed Hiroshima in Japan at the end of the Second World War.

In the small town of Parkfield, midway between Los Angeles and San Francisco, an earthquake occurs every 20 years. Cameras have been installed in a local bar in the town to record the event of the next earthquake. In San Francisco, scientists predict a strong possibility of a major earthquake occurring before the year 2020.

San Francisco, 1989

The focus of the 1989 earthquake was 18 km below the peak of Loma Prieta in the Santa Cruz Mountains. This was the 11th earthquake measuring 5.3 or more on the Richter Scale to strike the area of San Francisco Bay since 1865.

Recent earthquakes
1990

Peru (Richter Scale 5.8) 100 people killed and hundreds missing. Villages in the forest region of San Martín were flattened or swallowed up by landslides. Romania (Richter Scale 6.5-7.0) earthquake centred around town of Focsani, north-east of the capital Bucharest. About 70 people were killed, but the damage was limited as it was an intermediate-focus quake, occurring 100-150 km below the surface.
Philippines (Richter Scale 7.7) over 1,500 dead, 3,000 seriously injured and 110,000 homeless after an earthquake in northern Philippines. In the tourist resort of Baguio, hundreds of people were trapped under the rubble of collapsed buildings. 14 days after the first tremor, a man was rescued from beneath the rubble of a hotel.

1991

Pakistan (Richter Scale 6.8) 300 dead and 500 injured in North West Frontier Province. Severe damage to homes, roads, and power and telephone lines. Afghanistan (Richter Scale 6.5-6.8) epicentre in Hindu Kush Mountains, affecting remote villages of northern and eastern Afghanistan and killing 1,000 people. Central America (Richter Scale 7.5) earthquake in border area between Costa Rica and Panama destroyed thousands of homes, leaving 80 dead and 800 injured. Soviet Union (Richter Scale 7.2) in northern Georgia, earthquake caused damage in Republic's second largest city, Kutaisi, and in remote villages, leaving 100 dead.

First Australian quake

The first fatal earthquake (Richter Scale 5.5) ever recorded in Australia hit the town of Newcastle in New South Wales on 28 December 1989, killing 12 people and injuring 120.

GLOSSARY

aftershocks – extra movements of the ground which occur after the first shock waves.

crust – see lithosphere.

epicentre – the place on the Earth's surface directly above the focus of the earthquake.

fault – a weak point in the Earth's crust where the rock layers have ruptured and slipped.

focus – the point inside the Earth's crust where the shock waves of an earthquake are released.

lithosphere – the outer solid layer which surrounds the Earth. It consists of the crust and the upper mantle.

L (long) wave – a type of shock wave which travels along the surface during an earthquake and causes the most serious damage.

magma – the hot liquid rocks which lie beneath the Earth's crust.

mantle – the layer of rock which lies between the outer crust and the core of the Earth. The rocks in the upper mantle are in a semi-liquid state.

Mercalli Scale – a system used to measure the strength of an earthquake according to the amount of damage caused and the effects felt at the time of the tremors.

oceanic ridge – a type of plate boundary where new ocean floor is created by rising magma, which cools and hardens.

plate – one of the huge sections which make up the Earth's crust. The plates are continuously moving.

plate boundary – the place where two or more plates in the Earth's crust meet. Most earthquakes occur along plate boundaries.

P (primary) wave – a type of shock wave which is released from the focus of an earthquake. P waves are the fastest type of seismic wave.

Richter Scale – a system which measures the strength of an earthquake by using information recorded by a seismograph.

secondary tremor – violent trembling of the Earth's surface which is caused by surface, or L, waves and results in the most serious earthquake damage.

seismic wave – a huge burst of energy which is released from the rocks inside the Earth during an earthquake. Seismic waves are also called shock waves.

seismograph – an instrument which measures movements in the Earth's crust as wavy lines on a moving sheet of paper.

seismologist – a scientist who measures and studies shock waves to find out more about earthquakes.

shock wave – see seismic wave.

subduction zone – a type of plate boundary where part of the Earth's crust is destroyed as one plate is forced down beneath another.

S (secondary) wave – a type of shock wave which travels from the focus of the earthquake up to the surface.

transform fault – a type of plate boundary where two plates move against one another. Transform faults occur at right-angles to oceanic ridges.

tremor – a violent shaking of the ground caused by the shock waves from an earthquake.

tsunami – a huge sea wave caused by an earthquake occurring on the sea-bed. *Tsunamis* can be up to 30 m high.

INDEX

Photographic credits:

Cover, title page and pages 11, 13 both, 20, 21 top and middle, 23, 25 top right and bottom, 27 top right, middle and bottom and 29: Frank Spooner Pictures; pages 4-5, 12 left, 17 bottom, 27 top left and 28: Spectrum Colour Library; pages 12 right, 18, 24 and 25 top left: Science Photo Library; page 14: with kind permission from the Earthquake Research Institute of the University of Tokyo; page 15 top: The Ancient Art and Architecture Collection; pages 15 bottom and 17 top: Mary Evans Picture Library; pages 20-21: The Hutchison Library; page 26: Popperfoto.